D1067939

SPACE SCIENCE

SATURN

BY BETSY RATHBURN

BELLWETHER MEDIA ○ MINNEAPOLIS, MN

TM

Are you ready to take it to the extreme? Torque books thrust you into the action-packed world of sports, vehicles, mystery, and adventure. These books may include dirt, smoke, fire, and chilling tales. **WARNING**: read at your own risk.

This edition first published in 2019 by Bellwether Media, Inc.

Library of Congress Cataloging-in-Publication Data

Names: Rathburn, Betsy, author.
Title: Saturn / by Betsy Rathburn.
Description: Minneapolis, MN : Bellwether Media, Inc., [2019] | Series:
   Torque. Space Science | Audience: Ages 7-12. | Audience: Grades 3 to 7. |
   Includes bibliographical references and index.
Identifiers: LCCN 2018039173 (print) | LCCN 2018040774 (ebook) | ISBN
   9781681036960 (ebook) | ISBN 9781626179783 (hardcover : alk. paper)
Subjects: LCSH: Saturn (Planet)–Juvenile literature.
Classification: LCC QB671 (ebook) | LCC QB671 .R38 2019 (print) | DDC
   523.46–dc23
LC record available at https://lccn.loc.gov/2018039173

Editor: Kate Moening   Designer: Andrea Schneider

Printed in the United States of America, North Mankato, MN.

TABLE OF CONTENTS

RINGS IN THE SKY

Thousands of lights twinkle in the night sky. Each light is a planet or star many millions of miles away. But one holds an amazing surprise.

Through a **telescope**, a planet comes into view. Circling the planet is a series of beautiful **rings**. Some are even brighter than the planet itself. This is Saturn!

WHAT IS SATURN?

Saturn is one of the largest planets in the solar system. Only Jupiter is bigger. Saturn measures more than 72,000 miles (115,873 kilometers) across. This huge planet could fit more than 700 Earths inside it!

Through a telescope, Saturn looks pale yellow in color. Most of the planet has orange and tan stripes. But during winter, its north **pole** turns bright blue!

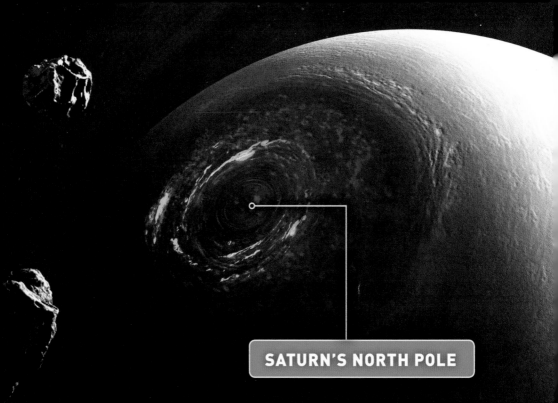

SATURN'S NORTH POLE

A TRICKY TRIP

Visiting Saturn would require strong spacecraft. Because the planet has no solid ground, no spacecraft can land there. Spacecraft must be able to fly into Saturn's atmosphere without being melted or crushed!

Saturn is a gas giant. Its **atmosphere** is mostly made of the gases hydrogen and helium. Layers of clouds swirl through the atmosphere.

Beneath the atmosphere, Saturn has no solid surface. Its center may contain a rocky **core** surrounded by liquid. Scientists must do more studies to know for sure.

Saturn is most famous for its bright rings. Seven large ring groups hold thousands of smaller rings. Some stretch more than 200,000 miles (321,869 kilometers) from the planet's center!

Each ring is made of many chunks of ice and rock. Most of these pieces are very small. Some are as big as a house. A few pieces are as big as mountains!

RINGS

HOW DID SATURN FORM?

Saturn formed about 4.6 billion years ago. The Sun spun in the middle of a cloud of gases and dust. This cloud was the solar nebula.

Eventually, gravity pulled the gas and dust into planets. Some of those materials became Saturn. This huge planet is made of the same gases as the Sun!

ILLUSTRATION OF
A SOLAR NEBULA

MANY MOONS

Saturn has at least 62 moons, but only 53 have been given names. One of the most famous is Enceladus. Some scientists believe it could hold life in the oceans below its frozen surface!

ENCELADUS

Some scientists think Saturn's rings are much younger than the planet. They may have formed when large, rocky objects nearby **collided**. Then, Saturn's strong gravity kept them in **orbit**.

CRATER

Like its rings, Saturn's moons were likely formed when nearby objects crashed into each other. Many of the planet's moons are covered in **craters**!

WHERE IS SATURN FOUND?

Saturn is the sixth planet from the Sun. It orbits the star from about 900 million miles (1.4 billion kilometers) away. One year on Saturn is 29 years on Earth!

A day on Saturn is much shorter than on Earth. It takes the planet less than 11 hours to complete one full spin.

FUN FACT

NO FUN IN THE SUN

Because of its distance from the Sun, Saturn is very cold. It is usually colder than -200 degrees Fahrenheit (-129 degrees Celsius)!

HOW FAR AWAY IS SATURN?

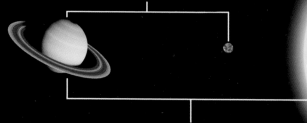

SATURN TO EARTH = 794,000,000 MILES
(1,278,000,000 KILOMETERS)

SATURN TO SUN = 887,000,000 MILES
(1,427,000,000 KILOMETERS)

WHY DO WE STUDY SATURN?

For now, there is no **evidence** of life beyond Earth. But scientists keep looking. They search for objects that may hold **bacteria** and other tiny life forms.

Some of Saturn's moons show signs of water. This could mean they hold life. The moons are too cold for humans. But they may hold other life forms!

ILLUSTRATION OF TITAN'S SURFACE

SATURN'S LARGEST MOON

Name: Titan

Discovered:
March 25, 1655
by Christiaan Huygens

Size: about 3,200 miles
(5,150 kilometers) across

Fast Facts:
- One of the most Earthlike places in the solar system
- Has a thick atmosphere and liquid on its surface
- May be home to living things

FUN FACT

TRAVEL BUDDIES

Cassini traveled to Saturn with another probe called *Huygens.* In 2005, *Huygens* landed on Titan, Saturn's largest moon. This was the first time humans landed a spacecraft on the moon of another planet!

Because Saturn is far away, scientists use **probes** to study it. A probe called *Cassini* orbited Saturn from 1997 to 2017. It took thousands of pictures of the planet and its moons.

Cassini also made new discoveries. It took the first photos of a huge storm on Saturn's north pole. It even discovered seven new moons!

CASSINI PROBE

GLOSSARY

atmosphere–the gases that surround Saturn and other planets

bacteria–very small living things; bacteria can usually only be seen with a microscope.

collided–crashed together

core–the innermost part of Saturn

craters–deep holes in the surface of a planet or other object

evidence–information used to show that something is true or false

gravity–the force that pulls objects toward one another

orbit–a complete movement around something in a fixed pattern

pole–one end of a planet or star; every planet or star has two poles.

probes–spacecraft designed to study faraway objects in space

rings–groupings of rocks or ice that circle a planet

solar nebula–a huge cloud of dust and gas left over from when the Sun formed

telescope–an instrument used to view distant objects in outer space

TO LEARN MORE

AT THE LIBRARY

Hamilton, John. *Cassini: Unlocking the Secrets of Saturn*. Minneapolis, Minn.: Abdo Publishing, 2018.

Radomski, Kassandra. *The Secrets of Saturn*. North Mankato, Minn.: Capstone Press, 2016.

Terp, Gail. *Saturn and Other Outer Planets*. Mankato, Minn.: Black Rabbit Books, 2019.

ON THE WEB

FACTSURFER

Factsurfer.com gives you a safe, fun way to find more information.

1. Go to www.factsurfer.com.

2. Enter "Saturn" into the search box.

3. Click the "Surf" button and select your book cover to see a

INDEX

The images in this book are reproduced through the courtesy of: Ezume Images, front cover; NAS/ JPL-Caltech/SSI/ Wikipedia, pp. 2, 8-9, 15; AstroStar, pp. 4-5 (boy/telescope); Andrey Prokhorov pp. 4-5 (sky/trees); Vadim Sadovski, pp. 6-7; Dotted Yeti, pp. 10-11, 16-17; Mopic, pp. 12-13; JPL-Caltech/SSI/ NASA Images, p. 14; Jurik Peter, pp. 18-19; NASA/JPL/ Wikipedia, pp. 20-21 (Cassini); Elenarts, pp. 20-21 (Saturn).